P9-CPY-194

1854

KIRSTEN'S CRAFT BOOK

*A Look at
Crafts from the
Past with Projects
You Can Make Today*

PLEASANT COMPANY PUBLICATIONS, INC.

Published by Pleasant Company Publications
© Copyright 1994 by Pleasant Company
All rights reserved. No part of this book may be used or reproduced
in any manner whatsoever without written permission except in the
case of brief quotations embodied in critical articles and reviews.
For information, address: Book Editor, Pleasant Company Publications,
8400 Fairway Place, P.O. Box 620998, Middleton, WI 53562.

First Edition.
Printed in the United States of America.
95 96 97 98 99 WCR 10 9 8 7 6 5

The American Girls Collection® and Kirsten®
are registered trademarks of Pleasant Company.

PICTURE CREDITS
The following individuals and organizations have generously
given permission to reprint illustrations in this book:
Page 1—The Bishop Hill Heritage Association; 4—Nordiska Museet; 5—Steven James
Carleson; 7—Keystone View Co.; 8—Everett B. Wilson; 9—Taken from *Natural Dyes*
by Sallie Pease Kierstead, Boston, Bruce, Humphries, Inc.; 10—Used with permission
of Sterling Publishing Co., Inc., 387 Park Ave. S., NY, NY, 10016, from *Create Your
Own Natural Dyes* by Kathleen Schultz, © 1975 by Sterling Publishing Co., Inc;
11—Reprinted with the permission of Macmillan Publishing Company from *Home Life
in Colonial Days* by Alice M. Earle. New York: Macmillan Publishing Company, 1922.
(top); Library of Congress (bottom); 12—*Early Pleasures and Pastimes*, Crabtree
Publishing Company, New York; 13—From the Permanent Collection of the Museum
of American Folk Art; 15—*Early Family Home*, Crabtree Publishing Company, 350
Fifth Ave., Suite 3308, New York, NY, 10118; 20, 21—*Early Settler Children*, Crabtree
Publishing Company, 350 Fifth Ave., Suite 3308, New York, NY, 10118; 23—*Early
Village Life*, Crabtree Publishing Company, 350 Fifth Ave., Suite 3308, New York,
NY, 10118; 25—Taken from *Paper Dolls* by Anne Tolstoi Wallach, © 1982;
27—Collection Betty Harvey-Jones; 28—Vesterheim Norwegian American Museum;
29—Old World Wisconsin, Eagle, WI; 31, 33—Nordiska Museet; 35—Natural History
Museum of Los Angeles County; 37—John Anderson Collection, Nebraska State
Historical Society; 39—Cranbrook Institute of Science.

Written and Edited by Jodi Evert
Designed and Art Directed by Jane S. Varda
Produced by Karen Bennett, Laura Paulini, and Pat Tuchscherer
Cover Illustration by Renée Graef
Inside Illustrations by Geri Strigenz Bourget
Photography by Mark Salisbury
Historical and Picture Research by Polly Athan,
Rebecca Sample Bernstein, Jodi Evert, and Doreen Smith
Crafts Made by Jean doPico, Kristi Jacobek, and June Pratt
Craft Testing Coordinated by Jean doPico
Prop Research by Leslie Cakora

All the instructions in this book have been tested by both children and adults.
Results from their testing were incorporated into this book. Nonetheless, all
recommendations and suggestions are made without any guarantees on the part of
Pleasant Company Publications. Because of differing tools, materials, conditions, and
individual skills, the publisher disclaims liability for any injuries, losses, or other
damages that may result from using the information in this book.

Library of Congress Cataloging-in-Publication Data
Kirsten's craft book : a look at crafts from the past with projects you can make today.
p. cm.—(The American girls collection)
ISBN 1-56247-112-0
1. Handicraft—Juvenile literature. 2. United States—Social life and customs—
19th century—Juvenile literature. [1. Handicraft. 2. United States—
Social life and customs—19th century.]
I. Series
TT171.K47   1994   680'.973'09034—dc20   94-8423   CIP   AC

CONTENTS

Special thanks to all the children and adults who tested the crafts and gave us their valuable comments:

Samantha Bechmann and her mother Sheila Bechmann
Emily Borne and her mother Rebecca Borne
Amanda Byrd and her mother Marcia Byrd
Jenna Eddington and her mother Sheri Eddington
Katie Hank and her mother Mary Pat Hank
Natalie Hegg and her mother Jill Hegg
Emily Holler and her mother Lana Holler
Amber Jackson and her mother Sally Jackson
Lindsey Jameson and her mother Sherry Lynn Schutz
Andrew and Lauren Johnson and their mother Christine Johnson
Tracy Juisto and her mother Jean Juisto
Shannon Kasten and her mother Judy Kasten
Erin Kelly and her mother Sally Kelly
Sharah King and her mother Ruth King
Taryn Knetter and her mother Traci Knetter
Kimberly Knothe and her mother Sharon Knothe
Leah Kolb and her mother Jill Cohen Kolb
Ellen Krahn and her mother Dawn Krahn
Nicole Kuehn and her mother Jill Kuehn
Sarah Langlois and her mother Valerie Langlois
Cassie Lee and her mother Debra Lee
Cathleen Lefferts and her mother Veronica Lefferts
Melissa Lindsay and her mother Patty Lindsay
Alicia and Madeline Lux and their mother Stephanie Stender
Laura Martin and her mother Denise Martin
Danielle Miles and her mother Dawn Miles
Nicole Miller and her mother Carol Miller
Katherine Murray and her mother Margaret Murray
Clara Neale and her mother Chris Neale
Jamie O'Connell and her mother Debbie O'Connell
Clarlie Rasmussen and her mother Faye Rasmussen
Ross Romenesko and his mother Tina Romenesko
Maria Swandby and her mother Toni Swandby
Leslie Thousand and her mother Debbie Thousand
Briony Varda and her mother Jane Varda
Sarah Verrill and her parents Kathleen and Steve Verrill

CRAFTS FROM THE PAST

Crafts like quilting and rug braiding were more than just pastimes for American girls long ago. In 1854, pioneer women like Kirsten and her mother had to make quilts and rugs themselves. The nearest town was hours away, so they went to the general store only a few times a year to get things that they couldn't make on their farm, like shoes and metal tools.

Pioneers wasted nothing. Things that we think are useless today were precious to them. Women and girls saved grease drippings and every scrap of fat to make soap and candles. They used wood ashes to scour their floors, made jelly from apple peels, and sewed grain bags into dishcloths. Women and girls did all these tasks by hand. There were no electric sewing machines or dishwashers on the frontier in 1854!

Some things have changed since Kirsten was growing up. Today's homes are lit by electric lights, not candles. People buy things like toys and clothes in stores instead of making them. But craftspeople today still make beautiful baskets, quilts, and clothing, just as pioneers did almost 150 years ago.

Learning how and why crafts were made long ago will help you understand what it was like to grow up the way Kirsten did. Making the crafts she might have made will bring history alive for you today.

KIRSTEN ♥ 1854

Kirsten Larson was a pioneer. She lived in a one-room log cabin on the Minnesota frontier. Kirsten and her family were from Sweden. They worked hard to make a good life in America. The Larsons sometimes longed for Sweden, but they never lost heart for the challenges of pioneer life.

Swedish woman using a spinning wheel.

CRAFT TIPS

This list of tips gives you some hints about creating the crafts in this book. But this is the most important tip: **work with an adult**. The best thing about these crafts is the fun you will have making them together.

1. Choose a time that suits you and the adult who's working with you, so that you will both enjoy making crafts together.

2. You can find most of the materials listed in this book in your home or at craft and fabric stores. If an item in the materials list is starred (*), look at the bottom of the list to find out where you can get it.

3. If you don't have something you need or can't find it at the store, think of something similar you could use. You might just think of something that works even better!

4. Read the instructions for a craft all the way through before you start it. Look at the pictures. They will help you understand the steps.

5. If there's a step that doesn't make sense to you, try it out with a piece of scrap paper or fabric first. Sometimes acting it out helps.

6. Select a good work area for your craft project. Pick a place that has plenty of light and is out of reach of pets and younger brothers and sisters.

PAINTS AND BRUSHES

*You'll use water-based, or **acrylic**, paints to make some of the crafts in this book. Here are a few hints for using paints and brushes:*

❤ *Don't dip your brush into the paint bottle. Squeeze a little paint onto newspaper or a paper plate.*

❤ *Have a bowl of water handy to clean the brush each time you change colors.*

❤ *Make sure one color is dry before adding another.*

❤ *Clean your brush with soap and water and let it dry before you put it away.*

7. Wear an apron, tie back your hair, and roll up your sleeves. Cover your work area with newspapers and gather all the materials you will need before you start.

8. It pays to be careful. Be sure to get an adult's help when the instructions tell you to. Have an adult help you use tools properly. Don't use the stove or oven without an adult's permission.

9. Pay attention when using sharp knives and scissors so you don't cut your fingers! Remember—good, sharp knives and scissors are safer and easier to use than dull ones.

10. To prevent spills, put the covers back on containers tightly. If you do spill, clean it up right away.

11. If your craft doesn't turn out exactly like the picture in the book, that's terrific! The pictures are there just to give you ideas. Crafts become more meaningful when you add your own personal touch.

12. Cleanup is part of making crafts, too. Leave your work area as clean as you found it. Wash and dry dishes, trays, and tabletops. Sweep the floor. Throw away the garbage.

THREADING A NEEDLE

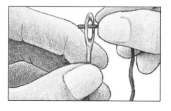

1. Wet the tip of the thread in your mouth. Then push the tip of the thread through the eye of the needle.

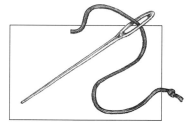

2. Pull about 5 inches of the thread through the needle. Then tie a double knot near the end of the long tail of thread.

A FRONTIER HOUSEHOLD

On chilly autumn evenings, Kirsten and her family sat around the dinner table, sharing their evening meal by candlelight. Kirsten and Mama made candles in the fall to get ready for the long, dark winter. Candle dipping was not one of Kirsten's favorite chores. She had to dip each candle about 25 times to make it thick enough to last one evening!

After supper, Kirsten helped Mama wash the dishes. Kirsten took a bucket of water that had been heated on the stove and poured it over a cake of homemade soap in the dishpan. Mama swished the water with her hands to make suds. The Larsons used this same kind of soap for washing laundry, bathing, and shaving.

When the dishes were finished, Kirsten and Mama joined Papa, Lars, and Peter around the wood stove. Papa taught the boys how to carve new handles for the family's tools and how to repair almost everything on the farm, from furniture to wheelbarrows.

Mama taught Kirsten how to spin raw wool into yarn. They dyed the yarn and then used it to knit wool stockings, mittens, caps, and scarves for the family. Mama also taught Kirsten to weave and braid warm rugs to cover the cabin floor. It was never too early to start making warm things for winter. In the wintertime, the cabin got so cold that sometimes Kirsten could see her breath when she woke up in the morning!

Kirsten loved sitting with her family around the wood stove each evening. Outside the cabin, wintry winds were already blowing the leaves from the trees. But inside, Kirsten and her family stayed snug and warm, listening to the hum of the spinning wheel, the steady click of knitting needles, and the crackle and pop of the fire.

A FRONTIER HOUSEHOLD

♥

Braided Mat

•

Dried Herbs and Flowers

•

Onion-Skin Dye

MAKING CANDLES

*Pioneers sometimes used a candle carousel to make the messy job of dipping candles go faster. Candles made from **tallow**, or boiled animal fat, gave off lots of smoke and smelled like frying grease when they burned. Beeswax candles burned bright and clear and smelled of honey.*

BRAIDED MAT

Braid a small mat for your favorite doll. Or keep braiding to make a bedside mat for yourself!

MATERIALS

9 fabric strips, each 1 inch wide and 3 feet long
Tape
Scissors
Heavy thread
Needle

DIRECTIONS

1. Tie 3 fabric strips together at 1 end in a knot. Tape the fabric strips to the table, just under the knot.

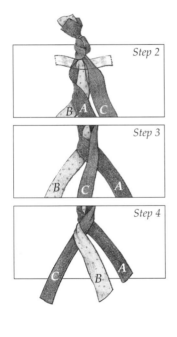

2. Braid the fabric strips together. Start on the left with strip A. Put A over B, so that A is in the middle.

3. Then put C over A, so that C is in the middle.

4. Now put B over C, so that B is in the middle. Keep braiding!

5. Stop braiding when there are 2 inches left. Tape the end of the braid to the table.

6. Cut an 18-inch piece of thread, and then thread the needle. Tie a double knot near the other end of the thread.

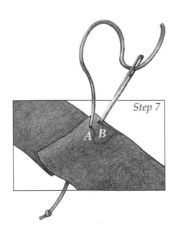

7. Backstitch 3 new strips of cloth to the 3 old strips. To backstitch, come up at A and go down at B.

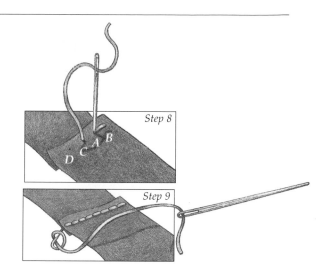

8. Come up at C. Then go down at A and come up at D. Keep stitching!

9. When you finish stitching, tie a knot close to your last stitch and cut off the extra thread. Untape the fabric strips.

10. Continue braiding and sewing the rest of the fabric strips together to make a long braid. Then tie a knot at the end of the braid.

11. Coil the braid around 1 of the end knots. This knot will be the center of your mat. Backstitch the braid to the knot.

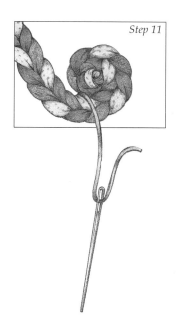

12. Keep coiling the braid around the center of the mat, stitching the new braid to the braid next to it every few inches.

13. When you've reached the knot at the other end of the braid, finish by stitching the knot to the underside of the mat. 💜

NOTHING WASTED

Pioneers believed that all things should be put to good use. Women and girls mended and patched clothing until it wore out. Then they used it for rags to scrub dishes and to make rugs. This woman is making a braided rug just as Kirsten and Mama did in the 1850s.

DRIED HERBS AND FLOWERS

A beautiful bouquet of dried flowers and herbs will last all winter.

MATERIALS

Fresh-picked herbs or flowers *(Roses, daisies, sage, and basil work well.)*
Piece of string or ribbon, 12 inches long

DIRECTIONS

1. Gather the herbs or flowers into a bouquet. Tie them together with string or ribbon near the bottoms of the stems.

2. Tie the ends of the string or ribbon together to make a loop.

3. Hang the flowers upside down in a dark, dry closet or attic. After a few weeks, your herbs or flowers will be dried.

4. Use your herbs to season foods, or hang them in the kitchen for decoration. Arrange your dried flowers in a vase, or use them to make the wreath on page 30. ♥

HERBAL REMEDIES

There weren't many doctors or druggists on the frontier. Pioneers like Kirsten and Mama made remedies from herbs they hung to dry from their cabin rafters. They used catnip for headaches, peppermint to calm the nerves, and mustard paste for chest colds.

ONION-SKIN DYE

MATERIALS

12 yards of cream-colored wool yarn
2 enamel cooking pots, 11½ quarts each
¼ cup of mild dish soap, such as Ivory®
Colander
Long-handled wooden spoon
1 tablespoon alum*
3 tablespoons cream of tartar*
Potholders
Towel
Large handful of onion skins*
*Available in grocery stores.

Dye made from onion skins gives wool a rich, golden glow.

DIRECTIONS

1. Let the yarn soak in a cooking pot of warm, soapy water for 30 minutes.

2. Place a colander over the drain in the kitchen sink. Ask an adult to help you pour the yarn and soapy water into the colander.

3. Rinse the yarn thoroughly under warm water.

4. Rinse the soap out of the cooking pot, and then fill it halfway with warm water. Ask an adult to help you move the pot to the stove.

ADDING A MORDANT

*When you mix in the alum and cream of tartar, they combine to make a **mordant**—a chemical solution that opens up the wool fiber so it can soak up dye.*

5. Stir in the alum and cream of tartar, and then add the yarn to the pot.

6. Let the mixture *simmer*, or bubble slightly, over low heat for 30 minutes. ➤

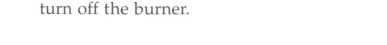

7. When the mixture has finished simmering, turn off the burner.

8. Ask an adult to pour the yarn and water into the colander.

Step 9

9. When the yarn is cool, squeeze out the water. Spread the damp yarn on a towel.

10. Wash and dry the cooking pot, and then add the onion skins. This will be your dye pot.

11. Fill the pot halfway with warm water, and ask an adult to help you take the pot to the stove.

12. Add the yarn to the dye pot. Let the yarn simmer over low heat for 30 minutes.

13. While the yarn is simmering, fill the other cooking pot halfway with water and ask an adult to help you take it to the stove. Let the water simmer over low heat.

14. Ask an adult to help you spoon the yarn out of the dye pot and into the pot of clear water.

COLORS FROM NATURE

Pioneers used all kinds of plants, fruits, nuts, and bark for dyes. Onion skins and goldenrod flowers created shades of yellow, tea and coffee created brown, and cranberries and wild black cherries created pink.

15. Let the yarn simmer for 30 minutes. Then turn off the burner and let the yarn cool for 15 minutes.

16. Ask an adult to pour the water and yarn into the colander in the sink. Rinse the yarn thoroughly, and then squeeze out the water.

17. Spread the yarn on a towel to dry. Then use it to make the yarn doll on page 22! ♥

Kirsten and Mama dyed wool in huge cast-iron kettles over outdoor fires, just as this woman is doing.

WASHING SHEEP

Before settlers sheared the wool from their sheep, they washed the sheep in wooden tubs or in a nearby stream. They used a water-and-tobacco solution to kill the bugs that lived in the sheep's wool.

A STITCH IN TIME

Pioneer mothers taught their daughters to sew at an early age so they could help make and mend clothes for the family. Kirsten stitched simple clothes, like aprons or baby clothes for her sister Britta, while Mama made more complicated dresses and shirts.

Pioneer women used wool, cotton, and linen cloth to make clothes. They made most of their cloth by hand, and they used every last scrap. If a pair of Papa's pants had too many holes to patch, Kirsten and Mama didn't throw them away. They cut them down and made them into a smaller pair of pants for Peter to wear. Then they saved the extra scraps of cloth in a ragbag.

Clothes weren't the only things Kirsten and Mama needed to sew. They also sewed their own dishtowels, blankets, pillowcases, pillows, and mattresses. They stuffed their pillows and mattresses by hand with cornhusks, straw, or feathers.

During recess at school, Miss Winston taught Kirsten and her friends how to sew a quilt. Kirsten had never quilted before. In Sweden, women wove their bedcovers on a loom.

Pioneer women sewed quilts for warmth, and the occasion for making them was special. Quilting parties, or *bees*, gave women a chance to get together with their friends. While they sewed, they traded stories and shared news about their families.

Sometimes women made quilts for friends who got married or were moving far away. They used scraps of fabric they had saved from their dresses and aprons, so each time their friend looked at the quilt, she would remember them.

A STITCH IN TIME

♥

Patchwork Pillow

•

Bunny Pincushion

•

Quilted Potholder

QUILTS TELL STORIES

One pioneer woman spent almost 25 years making a quilt that showed her whole life in pictures. She wrote in her diary, "I tremble when I remember what that quilt knows about me."

PATCHWORK PILLOW

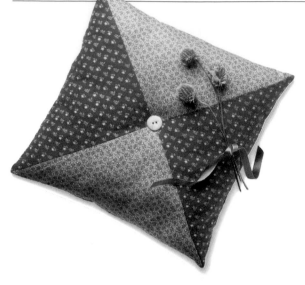

With this puffy pillow on your bed, you're sure to have sweet dreams.

MATERIALS

2 different-colored fabrics, each 8½ inches square
Fabric pen or pencil
Ruler
Scissors
Straight pins
Thread
Needle
Iron
Ironing board
11-inch fabric square
Polyester stuffing
Button

DIRECTIONS

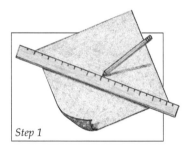

Step 1

1. Lay an 8½-inch fabric square on the table with the *right side,* or front side, facing down. Use the fabric pen or pencil and ruler to draw a line from the top left corner of the square to the bottom right corner.

2. Cut along the line. You will end up with 2 fabric triangles. Make 2 triangles out of the other 8½-inch fabric square in the same way.

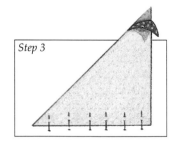

Step 3

3. Put 1 triangle of each fabric together, with the right sides facing each other. Pin the triangles together along 1 of the short edges as shown.

4. Cut an 18-inch piece of thread, and then thread the needle. Tie a double knot near the other end of the thread.

5. Sew running stitches ¼ inch from the triangle's edge. To make running stitches, come up at A and go down at B.

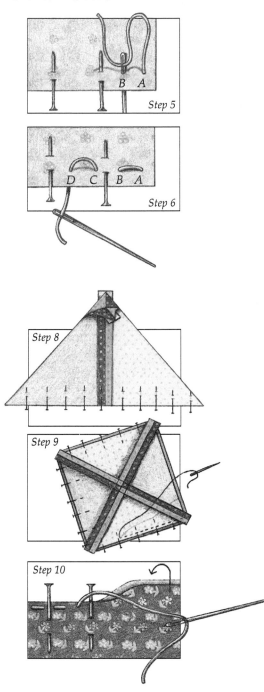

Step 5

6. Then come up at C and go down at D. When you finish stitching, tie a knot close to your last stitch and cut off the extra thread.

Step 6

7. Remove the pins. Follow steps 3 through 6 to sew together the other 2 fabric triangles. Then ask an adult to iron the seams flat.

8. Pin the right sides of the sewn triangles together along 1 edge. Sew them together with running stitches. Ask an adult to iron the seam flat.

Step 8

9. Pin the 11-inch fabric square to the patchwork square on 3 sides, with the right sides together. Then sew running stitches along these edges. Make smaller stitches at the corners.

Step 9

10. Unpin the fabric. Turn the pillow inside out and fill it with stuffing. Fold in the last edge and pin it together. Sew the pillow closed.

Step 10

11. Unpin the edge. Sew on a button in the very center through all the layers of the pillow. 🖤

CORNHUSK MATTRESSES

Pioneers had fun husking corn after each fall's corn harvest. Then women like Mama and Kirsten dried the cornhusks in the sun, shredded them by hand, and stuffed them into mattress coverings, which were often made of itchy burlap.

BUNNY PINCUSHION

*This plump little bunny
makes a perfect pincushion.*

MATERIALS

Pencil
Sheet of tracing paper
Scissors
Straight pins
Piece of cotton fabric, 10 inches square
Ruler
Thread
Needle
Cotton balls
Felt
Fabric glue
3 small buttons

DIRECTIONS

1. Use a pencil to trace the 2 oval patterns shown on page 42 onto tracing paper. Cut out the ovals.

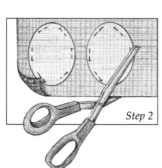
Step 2

2. Pin the ovals onto the *wrong side*, or back side, of the fabric and cut around the edges. Unpin the patterns.

3. Lay 1 fabric oval on the table, with the *right side*, or front side, facing up.

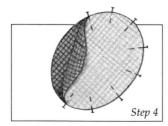
Step 4

4. Lay the other oval on top, with the wrong side facing up. Pin the edges of the 2 ovals together.

5. Cut an 18-inch piece of thread, and then thread the needle. Tie a double knot near the other end of the thread.

6. Backstitch the ovals together, ¼ inch from the edge. To backstitch, come up at A and then go down at B.

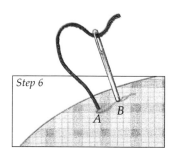
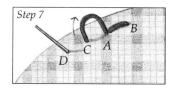

7. Come up at C. Then go down at A and come up at D.

8. Keep stitching until there are 1½ inches left open. Then tie a knot close to your last stitch and cut off the extra thread.

9. Unpin the fabric and turn it inside out. Stuff the pincushion with cotton balls until it's plump.

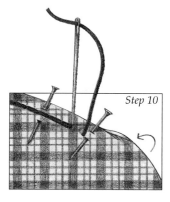

10. Tuck the raw edges of fabric inside the pincushion. Pin the edges together and finish backstitching the edge.

11. Remove the pins. Use the pattern shown on page 42 to make felt ears for your bunny pincushion. Then glue on the ears, button eyes and a nose, felt whiskers, and a cotton-ball tail. ❤

From the book Happy Birthday, Kirsten!

STITCHING FOR FUN

Pioneer girls practiced their stitches by making simple toys or clothes for their dolls. They also had fun making quilts, as Kirsten and her friends did. Some girls learned how to sew when they were only four years old!

QUILTED POTHOLDER

*Make a pretty potholder
to brighten the kitchen.*

MATERIALS

Pencil
Sheet of tracing paper
2 pieces of cotton fabric, each 8 inches square
8-inch square of fabric tracing paper *(Dritz® Mark-B-Gone
is one brand.)*
Ballpoint pen
Cotton batting, $7\frac{1}{2}$ inches square
Straight pins
Scissors
Ruler
Quilting thread
Needle
Piece of yarn, 5 inches long

DIRECTIONS

1. Use the pencil to trace the quilt square pattern shown on page 43 onto tracing paper. Don't cut out the pattern.

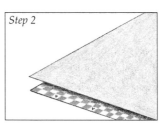

2. Lay 1 piece of fabric on the table, with the *right side*, or front side, facing up. Then lay the square of fabric tracing paper on top of the fabric.

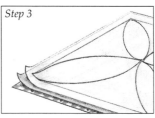

3. Center the tracing-paper quilt square, design side up, on top of the fabric tracing paper. Trace the pattern firmly with a ballpoint pen.

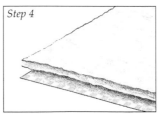

4. Lay the other piece of cotton fabric on the table, with the *wrong side*, or back side, facing up. Then lay the batting on top.

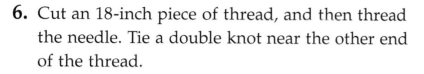

5. Place the other piece of fabric on top of the batting, design side up. Pin the edges of these 3 layers together.

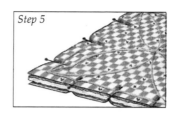
Step 5

6. Cut an 18-inch piece of thread, and then thread the needle. Tie a double knot near the other end of the thread.

7. Backstitch along the lines of the pattern. To backstitch, come up at A and go down at B.

8. Come up at C. Then go down at A and come up at D. When the pattern is finished, tie a knot close to your last stitch and cut off the extra thread.

9. Unpin the edges of the fabric. Then fold in the raw edges, pinning them together as you go.

10. Whipstitch around the outside of the potholder, starting about 1 inch from 1 corner. To whipstitch, come up at A. Stitch over the edge of the fabric and come up at B.

11. Stop stitching when there are 2 inches left open. Unpin the edges. Make a loop with the 5-inch piece of yarn and slip the ends into the potholder.

12. Fold in the raw edges, pin them together, and finish whipstitching. Your stitches will hold the loop in place. Then unpin the edges, and your potholder is finished! ❤

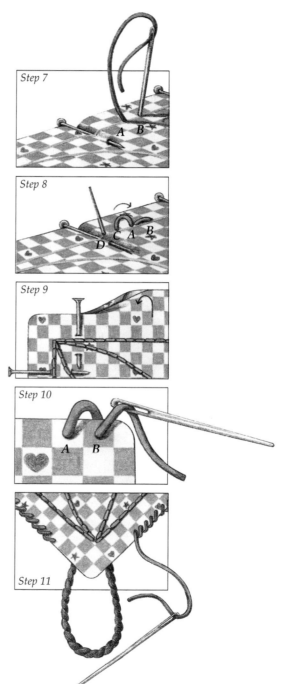
Step 7

Step 8

Step 9

Step 10

Step 11

PIONEER PLAYTHINGS

Busy pioneer children like Kirsten had lots of work to do, but they still found ways to have fun. Early in the morning, Kirsten went out to the barn to gather eggs for breakfast. The chickens laid eggs all around the barn—it was fun to try to find them hidden in the hay. If Kirsten was lucky, she might be able to watch a chick hatch from its egg!

After breakfast, Kirsten helped Mama clean up and keep an eye on baby Britta. If Britta was fussy, Kirsten quieted her with the little yarn doll she had made, or she twirled a chromatrope toy over the baby's head. Britta loved to watch the changing colors.

In the fall, Kirsten helped with the harvest. There were apples to pick and corn to husk. When the work was finished, Kirsten and her cousins Anna and Lisbeth made corncob puppets and apple-head dolls. Sometimes they even bobbed for apples!

After the harvest, it was time to go back to school. At recess, Kirsten loved to play tree tag. In tag, it didn't matter that she couldn't speak English very well. She was a very fast runner! On the way home from school, Kirsten, Anna, and Lisbeth sometimes stopped to swing on a pasture gate or to play in their secret fort under the cherry tree. They played school with their dolls and pretended to feed them little mud cakes decorated with gooseberries, acorn caps, or sunflower seeds.

In the wintertime, Kirsten sometimes helped her brother Lars work the trap line. It was cold work, but Kirsten kept warm by swooshing along on top of the snow in her snowshoes. When the streams froze solid, she and her brothers loved to play sliding games across the ice. They took turns to see who could slide the farthest and the fastest!

PIONEER PLAYTHINGS

♥

Yarn Doll

•

Chromatrope Toy

•

Magic Wallet

SIMPLE PLEASURES

There were no televisions or radios in 1854. Pioneer children made their own fun with things they found in the meadows and woods near their homes. They made stepping-stone bridges across streams, wove flower chains, and played in fall leaves.

YARN DOLL

MATERIALS

12 yards of yarn
Piece of cardboard, 7 inches by 5 inches
7 pieces of yarn, each 5 inches long
Scissors
Styrofoam® or rubber ball, 1 inch wide
Fabric glue
3 small buttons, about $\frac{1}{4}$ inch wide
Bits of ribbon and yarn for hair and mouth

This pretty yarn doll is simple to make.

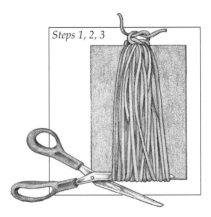

Steps 1, 2, 3

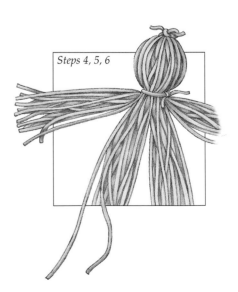

Steps 4, 5, 6

DIRECTIONS

1. Wrap the yarn around the piece of cardboard the long way. Then take a short piece of yarn and slip it under the wrapped yarn.

2. Pull the short piece of yarn to the top of the cardboard. Tie all the yarn together tightly with a double knot.

3. Cut off the ends of the short piece of yarn close to the knot. Then cut the yarn open at the bottom of the cardboard.

4. Place the yarn over the small ball. Arrange the yarn so it covers the ball completely.

5. Use another short piece of yarn to tie the yarn together at the bottom of the ball. Cut off the ends of the short piece of yarn close to the knot.

6. To make your doll's body and arms, divide the rest of the yarn into 4 equal sections.

7. Use 2 short pieces of yarn to tie the outer sections of yarn halfway down. Cut off the ends of the short pieces of yarn close to the knots.

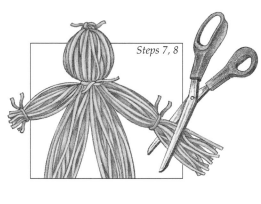

Steps 7, 8

8. Cut off the yarn a little below the knots. You've just made your doll's arms!

9. Tie the 2 middle sections together about $\frac{1}{3}$ of the way down with a short piece of yarn. Cut off the ends of the short piece of yarn close to the knot.

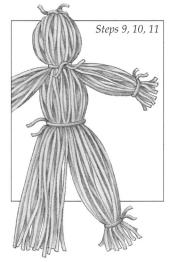

Steps 9, 10, 11

10. Make your doll's legs by dividing the remaining yarn into 2 equal sections.

11. Tie each section near the bottom with a small piece of yarn. Then cut off the ends of the short pieces of yarn.

12. Glue on button eyes and a nose and yarn hair and a mouth. Add hair ribbons, and your doll is ready to play! ❤

YARN FROM SHEEP

This man is shearing a sheep the same way pioneers sheared sheep in the 1850s. Pioneers usually sheared sheep in the early spring, when the coldest weather was over. After shearing, the wool was **carded***, or untangled with brushes, and spun into yarn.*

CHROMATROPE TOY

Another name for this toy was "The Philosophical Whizgig"!

MATERIALS

Pencil
Sheet of tracing paper
Newspaper
Sheet of white drawing paper
Crayons or markers
Scissors
Piece of poster board, 5 inches square
Glue
Piece of string, 3 feet long

DIRECTIONS

1. Use a pencil to trace the chromatrope patterns shown on page 44 onto tracing paper. Don't cut them out.

2. Place the sheet of tracing paper onto newspaper, design side down.

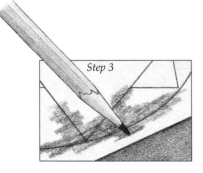

3. Use the side of the pencil to color over the backs of the circles.

4. Place the tracing paper on top of the sheet of drawing paper, design side up. Then draw over the lines of both circles, pressing firmly.

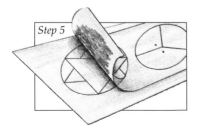

5. Lift up the tracing paper. The pencil markings from the back of the tracing paper will come off where you traced.

6. Color the circles with crayons or markers. Then cut them out.

7. Place 1 of the circles onto the piece of poster board. Trace the circle onto the poster board and cut it out.

8. Glue 1 of the circles, colored side out, to 1 side of the poster-board circle. Then glue the other circle, colored side out, to the other side.

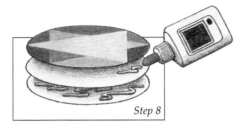

Step 8

9. When the glue dries, use the tip of your scissors to punch the 2 holes near the center of the circle.

10. Thread the ends of the string through the holes. Then tie the ends together in a double knot.

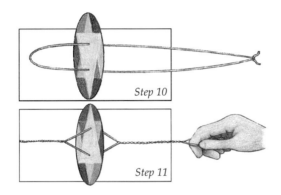

Step 10

Step 11

11. Pick up the string by both ends, and slide the circle to the middle. Swing the circle over and over until the string is tightly wound.

12. Practice pulling your hands apart slowly to make the circle spin. Watch for the changing colors and patterns! ♥

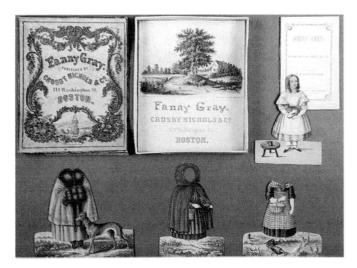

PAPER ON THE FRONTIER

In 1854, paper was made from linen or cotton rags, and it was expensive. Pioneers sold their worn-out cotton rags to a ragman. Then the rags were made into paper. Paper toys, like this colorful set of Fanny Gray paper dolls, would have been a special delight to a pioneer child.

MAGIC WALLET

*Make money jump from one side of
this mysterious wallet to the other!*

MATERIALS

Fine sandpaper (150 grit)
2 blocks of wood, 6 inches long, 3 inches wide,
   and $1/2$ inch thick*
Foam paintbrush, 1 inch wide
Acrylic paint, any color
Hammer
8 flathead thumbtacks
2 pieces of $3/8$-inch grosgrain ribbon, each 5 inches long
2 pieces of $3/8$-inch grosgrain ribbon, each 6 inches long
Scissors
Available in hardware and lumber stores.

DIRECTIONS

1. Sand the wood blocks until they are smooth. Then wipe off the dust.

2. Use the foam paintbrush to paint 1 side of each wood block with acrylic paint.

3. When the paint is dry, turn the wood blocks over to paint another side.

4. Keep painting until the wood blocks are painted on all sides. Add a second coat of paint if necessary.

5. Ask an adult to help you use a hammer to gently tack 1 end of each *5-inch* ribbon to the edge of 1 of the wood blocks. Lay the ribbons across the block.

Step 5

6. Now tack 1 end of each *6-inch* ribbon to the opposite edge of the same wood block. Cross the ribbons and lay them across the block.

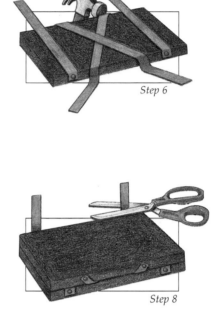

Step 6

7. Place the other wood block on top of the first wood block, with the ribbons in the middle. Let the ribbon tails hang out from the sides.

8. Tack all 4 ribbons to the edges of the top block of wood as shown. Trim off the extra ribbon.

Step 8

9. Now you're ready to amaze your friends and family with the magic wallet trick! Open your magic wallet and lay it on a table.

10. Place a dollar bill under the ribbons on the right half of the wallet.

Step 10

11. Close the right half of the wallet over the left half.

Step 11

12. Now open the wallet to the left. The dollar bill will have magically jumped to the other side! ❤

Step 12

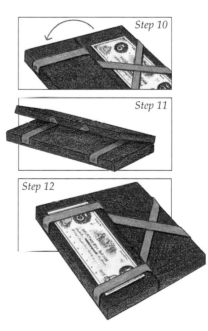

HANDMADE TOYS

Most children who lived on the frontier had only handmade toys. In many pioneer homes, grandparents taught their grandchildren how to make simple toys out of wood scraps. Children had as much fun making the toys as they had playing with them!

SWEDISH TRADITIONS

Kirsten and her family made a good life for themselves in America. They had good friends, a comfortable home, and plenty of food to eat. But sometimes Kirsten still longed for Sweden. It helped to look around the cabin at the things from Sweden—and to keep alive Swedish traditions.

When the Larsons left Sweden, they had to fit everything they needed for their new life into two big trunks. They packed clothes, blankets, tools, and food for the trip. Kirsten could bring only a few things that were most precious to her. She chose things that reminded her of Sweden and the people she loved—a hand-painted trinket box, hair ribbons that Mormor, her grandmother, had woven for her, and of course her beloved doll Sari.

On the frontier, Kirsten and her family kept some of their Swedish traditions alive. At Christmastime, Mama and Kirsten hung woven wall hangings and decorated their holiday tables with straw figures and painted horses, just as they had in Sweden.

The Larsons decorated their home with branches and wildflowers to celebrate Midsummer. Today, Midsummer is celebrated on June 24. In Sweden, this day is so long that the sun stays out all night! Everyone wants to be outside picnicking, singing, and dancing around a maypole. Young girls pick seven different kinds of wildflowers and place them underneath their pillows. When they go to sleep, they hope to dream about which boy they will marry someday.

Whenever Kirsten was homesick for Sweden, it helped to remember what Mormor had told her when they said good-bye. Mormor said, "When you're lonely, look at the sun. Remember that we all see the same sun."

SWEDISH TRADITIONS

♥

Midsummer Wreath

•

Dala Horse

•

Stenciled Box

MAYPOLES

Dancing around a maypole to celebrate Midsummer is an old Swedish custom that is still practiced today. Swedish maypoles are covered with greens and flowers, and so are many other things during the Midsummer celebration— houses, cars, and even boats!

MIDSUMMER WREATH

Wildflower wreaths decorate maypoles on Midsummer—a day when the sun doesn't set in Sweden!

MATERIALS

Bundle of reeds, 1 inch thick and 2 feet long*
Roasting pan
Paper towels
Twine
Scissors
Piece of ribbon, 5 feet long
Dried flowers *(See page 8 to dry your own.)*
Extra ribbon for bows
*Available in craft stores and basket supply stores.

DIRECTIONS

1. Soak the reeds in a roasting pan of warm water until they're flexible, about 15 minutes.

2. Dry the excess water from the reeds, and then bend them into a circle, overlapping the ends.

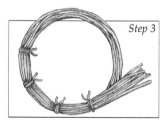

3. Have a partner help you tie the reeds together with twine. Tie tight double knots, and then cut off the extra twine.

4. Let the reeds dry for about 15 minutes, and then tie 1 end of the 5-foot ribbon around the wreath.

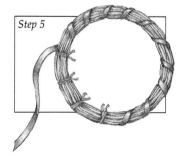

5. Wrap the ribbon loosely around the wreath. Leave gaps so that the reeds show through.

6. Cut the flower stems to 3 inches. Weave the flowers into the wreath, or tie them on with ribbon. Add ribbon bows, and your wreath is finished! ❤

DALA HORSE

MATERIALS

Self-hardening clay
Paintbrush, 1 inch wide
Acrylic paints *(red, blue, black, and white)*
Small artist's paintbrush

Colorful toy horses with traditional painted designs are a handicraft from Dalarna, Sweden.

DIRECTIONS

1. Model a small horse out of clay. Form the body by rolling a small oval shape about the size of an egg.

2. Then attach legs and a neck and head. Let your clay horse harden overnight.

3. Use the 1-inch paintbrush to give the horse a base coat of red paint. After the paint is dry, add a second coat if necessary.

4. Finish your Dala horse by adding traditional painted designs in blue, black, and white with the artist's paintbrush. ♥

TRAVELING HORSES

This woman from Dalarna, Sweden, is painting beautiful toy horses just as her ancestors did in Kirsten's time. In the 1850s, people from Dalarna traveled all over Sweden to sell them. As they traveled, they stayed overnight at farm homes along the way. They often left painted horses as gifts for the children.

STENCILED BOX

*Swedish girls kept small trinkets
in beautiful hand-painted boxes.*

MATERIALS

Pencil
Piece of tracing paper, 3 inches square
Scissors
Unfinished oval wooden box with lid, 3 inches by 4 inches
2 sheets of white drawing paper
Fine sandpaper (150 grit)
Foam paintbrush, 1 inch wide
Acrylic paints *(light blue, white, green, and black)*
Stencil brush
Red stencil paint
Tape
Small artist's paintbrush

DIRECTIONS

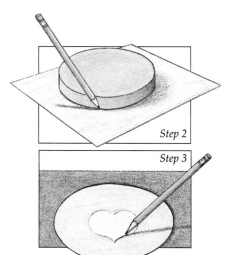

1. To make the stencil, trace the heart shape shown
on page 44 onto tracing paper and cut it out.

2. Lay the box lid onto a sheet of drawing paper.
Trace around the lid and then cut out the
oval shape.

Step 2

Step 3

3. Center the heart in the middle of the lid pattern.
Trace the heart onto the paper.

4. Carefully cut the heart shape out of the lid
pattern. Begin cutting in the middle of the
heart, and work your way out to the edges.
You've finished making your stencil!

5. Lightly sand your wooden box and lid. Wipe
away the dust.

6. Use the foam paintbrush to paint the outside of the box and the lid light blue. Let the paint dry for 15 minutes. Add a second coat of paint if necessary.

7. To practice painting your stencil, lay it onto the other sheet of drawing paper.

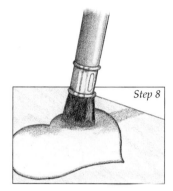

Step 8

8. Rub the stencil brush over the red stencil paint. Hold the brush upright, and gently paint around the edge of the heart. Then fill in the middle.

9. Slowly remove the stencil and let the paint around the edge of the stencil dry completely.

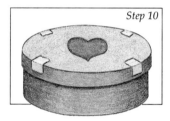

Step 10

10. Then place your stencil onto the box lid. Tape the edges of the stencil to the lid.

11. Stencil the heart onto the box lid, just as you have practiced. Then remove the stencil and let the paint dry.

12. Finish your stenciled box by adding green leaves and white and black accents with the artist's paintbrush. 🖤

PAINTED TRUNKS

*Huge wooden trunks were often decorated with **rosemaling**, beautiful floral designs that were traditional in Sweden and other Scandinavian countries. In Sweden, the trunks were sometimes painted by traveling artists, who carried news and stories from town to town.*

ARTS FROM THE INDIANS

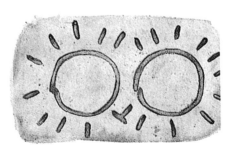

S ome pioneers believed Indians were savages, bloodthirsty and wild. Kirsten didn't know what to believe, until she met a real Indian girl named Singing Bird.

At first, Kirsten and Singing Bird couldn't speak each other's languages, so they talked by drawing pictures. If Singing Bird drew two full suns, it meant she wanted to meet Kirsten in two days. Many Indian people who lived on the Plains used picture symbols to keep track of time and to mark special events. They painted symbols on bark, stones, or animal skins. On these calendars, years were known as *winters*, and each year was made up of *moons* instead of months.

Plains Indians lived in all kinds of houses—wigwams, earth lodges, and tepees. Singing Bird made a tiny tepee from leaves and twigs to show Kirsten what her home looked like. Real tepees were usually made by Indian women. The women chose the sites, and then they wrapped animal-skin covers around a frame of 25-foot poles.

Making a tepee cover was often like a pioneer quilting bee. If a woman needed a new tepee cover, she invited her friends to a feast. After the feast, they made a new cover. Some women cut the skins and others sewed them together. Indian children sometimes made playhouses from old tepee covers and poles. That way, young girls like Singing Bird could begin to learn how to make tepees.

Indian girls also learned to sew their own clothes, pouches, and moccasins. And they helped the women cook, carry water, and gather wood. Some Indian families marked their firewood and other belongings with decorated owner sticks. Each stick had its own design, and it meant that no one outside the family could take or touch what it marked!

ARTS FROM THE INDIANS

♥

Leather Pouch

•

Clay Bead Necklace

•

Calendar Stick

•

Owner Stick

BUFFALO

When Indians killed a buffalo, they used every part of it. They made the hair into rope and dried the stomach to use as a cooking vessel. Indian men and women often painted buffalo hides. They believed that the hide still held the buffalo's spirit. By painting the hide, they honored the animal's spirit.

LEATHER POUCH

This pouch is perfect for tying around your waist or slinging over your shoulder.

MATERIALS

Piece of chamois, 12 inches square*
Dinner plate, about 12 inches wide
Fabric pen with disappearing ink
Scissors
Ruler
Leather thong, 4½ feet long
2 wooden beads, each ½ inch wide
Pencil
Paper
Small artist's paintbrush
Acrylic paints, any colors
Thread
Needle
Small colored beads
Available in the automotive section of department stores.

DIRECTIONS

1. Lay the chamois on the table. Place the dinner plate on the chamois, and use the fabric pen to trace around it. Cut out the circle.

2. Mark an even number of dots 1 inch from the outer edge of your circle, about 1 inch apart.

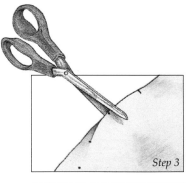

3. Cut a tiny slit on each marked dot. To cut a slit, fold in the edge of the chamois so the dot shows on the fold. Then cut a small slit on the dot.

Step 3

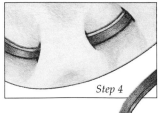

4. Weave the leather thong in and out of the slits around the edge of the chamois.

Step 4

5. Tie a knot 3 inches from each end of the thong. Slip a wooden bead onto each end of the thong, and then tie another knot after each bead.

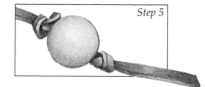

Step 5

6. Pull the beads to close the pouch. Notice that the middle of the circle becomes the bottom of your pouch. Then open your pouch and lay it on the table, with the outside facing up.

7. Plan a design for your pouch on paper. Then use the fabric pen to draw the design on your pouch. Paint your design any colors you like.

8. To add bead stitching, cut a piece of thread that is 18 inches long. Thread the needle and tie a double knot near the other end of the thread.

9. Bring the needle up at A, and then string 3 or 4 beads onto the thread.

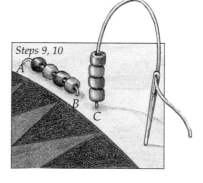

Steps 9, 10

10. Go down at B and come up at C. Keep stitching!

11. When you finish stitching, tie a knot on the underside of the leather close to your last stitch. Cut off the extra thread, and your pouch is finished! ❤

INDIAN PAINTS AND BRUSHES

Indian men and women sometimes painted themselves for decoration, to frighten enemies, or to protect their skin from the sun and wind. They made paintbrushes by chewing on the ends of willow twigs or by tying animal hair to the end of a stick. In the 1850s, many Indians also painted calendars called **winter counts,** *just as this man is doing.*

CLAY BEAD NECKLACE

Many Indians made necklaces out of claws, beaks, nuts, berries, bones, and clay beads. Paint yours with your favorite colors.

MATERIALS

Self-hardening clay
Toothpicks
Piece of cardboard, 4 inches square
Small artist's paintbrush
Acrylic paints, any colors
Scissors
Dental floss
Ruler
Needle

INSTRUCTIONS

1. Form beads with clay. It's best to keep the beads small, but they can be any shape.

2. Pierce each bead with a toothpick while the clay is still soft.

3. Let the beads harden overnight. As they harden, they will shrink.

4. Make a stand to paint your beads. Roll a small piece of clay into a ball and press it onto the cardboard square. This will be the base of your stand.

5. Then push a toothpick into the clay base. Place a hardened bead onto the end of the toothpick. Paint the bead with acrylic paints.

6. After a few minutes, the paint will be dry. Keep painting until all the beads are painted.

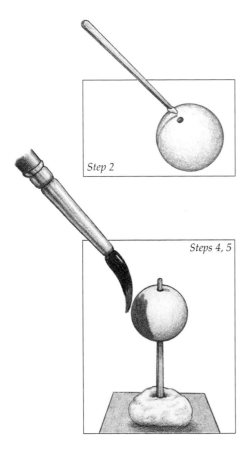

Step 2

Steps 4, 5

7. To make the beads into a necklace, cut a 3-foot piece of dental floss.

8. Thread the needle with dental floss. Tie a double knot 2 inches from the other end of the floss.

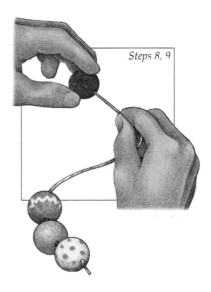

Steps 8, 9

9. Use the needle to string your clay beads onto the floss.

10. Stop stringing beads when there are 3 inches of floss left.

11. Tie a double knot at this end of the floss as close to the beads as possible.

12. Then tie the two ends of floss together in a double knot. Your necklace is ready to wear! ♥

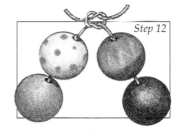

Step 12

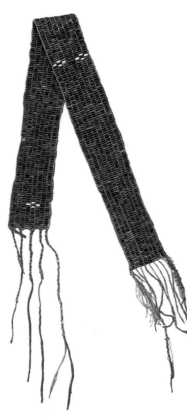

WAMPUM

*Many Indians used shell beads called **wampum** as money. The beads were either white or purple. Purple beads were worth twice as much as white beads. Wampum beads were often made into belts or strung on thread. Some Indian men tattooed the insides of their forearms with sets of lines for measuring wampum strands.*

CALENDAR STICK

This calendar gives you a whole year of memories in pictures.

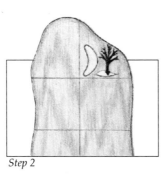

Step 2

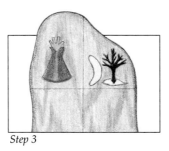

Step 3

MATERIALS

Pencil
Ruler
Flat board, 2 feet long and 4 inches wide
Small artist's paintbrush
Acrylic paints, any colors
Hammer
Nail
Piece of leather thong, 6 inches long

DIRECTIONS

1. Lightly draw a line down the middle of the board. Then draw 11 light lines across the board, 2 inches apart.

2. Decide what month you want to draw first. Draw a moon, which is an Indian symbol for "month," in the first box on the right side. Then draw a symbol for the current month next to the moon. Paint your symbols.

3. At the end of the month, draw a symbol for a special event that happened that month in the first box on the left side of the board. Then paint the symbol.

4. Erase the pencil lines around the symbols you've drawn. Continue to add symbols each month.

5. Ask an adult to hammer a hole through the top of the board. Thread the thong through the hole and tie it together to make a loop. ♥

OWNER STICK

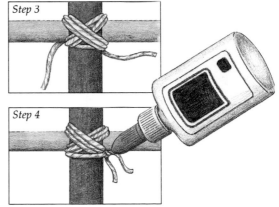

MATERIALS

Small artist's paintbrush
Acrylic paints, any colors
3-foot wooden dowel, $\frac{1}{2}$ inch wide
2-foot wooden dowel, $\frac{5}{16}$ inch wide
Scissors
Ruler
Twine
Glue
1-foot wooden dowel, $\frac{5}{16}$ inch wide
Feathers

Place your owner stick near something that belongs to you—a bookshelf, a box of toys, or even the door to your room!

DIRECTIONS

1. Begin by painting the dowels. When the paint dries, form a cross with the 3-foot dowel and the 2-foot dowel.

2. Then cut a 3-foot piece of twine. Tie 1 end of the twine around the 3-foot dowel as shown.

3. With a partner, wind the twine crossways a few times in 1 direction, and then in the other. Stop winding when there are 3 inches left.

4. Wrap the twine loosely around the 3-foot dowel once, and then tie the twine in a tight double knot. Squeeze a little glue onto the knot to help hold it in place.

5. Now tie the 1-foot dowel a few inches below the 2-foot dowel in the same way. Tie feathers to the ends of the crossbars, and your owner stick is finished! ❤

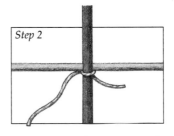

Step 2

Step 3

Step 4

PATTERNS

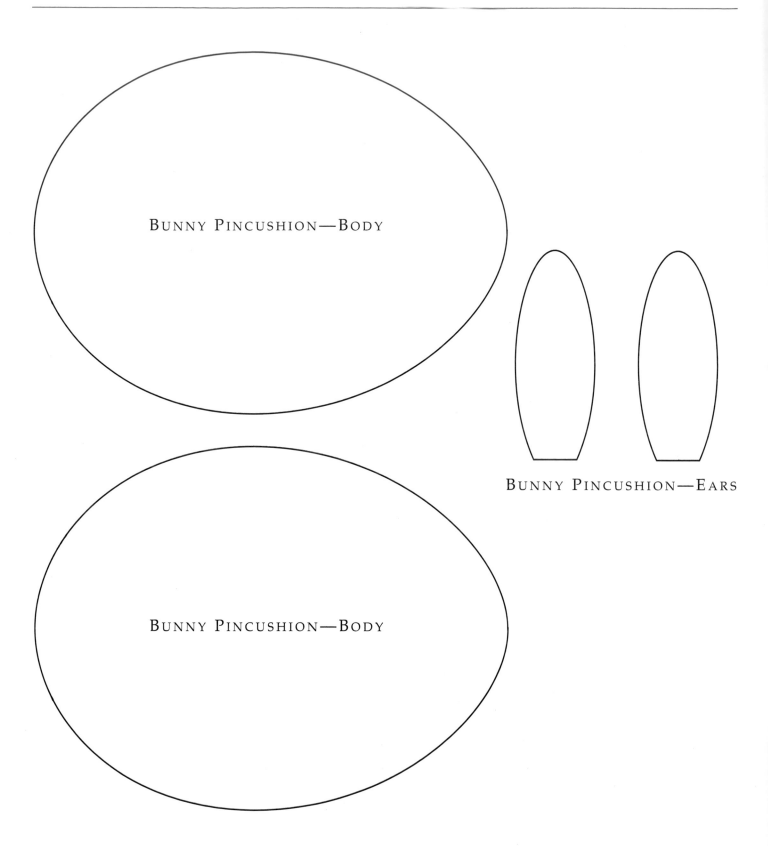

BUNNY PINCUSHION—BODY

BUNNY PINCUSHION—EARS

BUNNY PINCUSHION—BODY

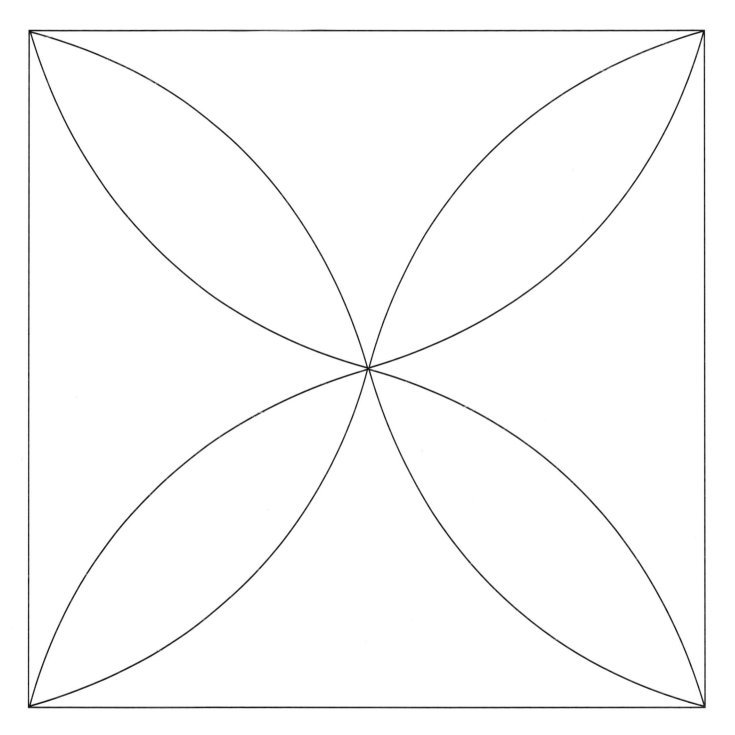

QUILTED POTHOLDER

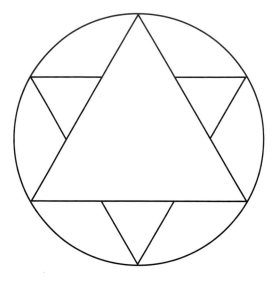

CHROMATROPE TOY—FRONT

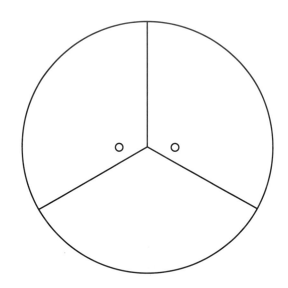

CHROMATROPE TOY—BACK

STENCILED BOX

AMERICAN GIRLS PASTIMES™
Activities from the Past for Girls of Today

You'll enjoy all the Pastimes books about your favorite characters in The American Girls Collection®.

Learn to cook foods that Felicity, Kirsten, Addy, Samantha, and Molly loved with the Pastimes **COOKBOOKS.** They're filled with great recipes and fun party ideas.

Make the same crafts that your favorite American Girls character made. Each of the **CRAFT BOOKS** has simple step-by-step instructions and fascinating historical facts.

Imagine that you are your favorite American Girls character as you stage a play about her. Each of the **THEATER KITS** has four Play Scripts and a Director's Guide.

Learn about fashions of the past as you cut out the ten outfits in each of the **PAPER DOLL KITS.** Each kit also contains a make-it-yourself book plus historical fun facts.

There are **CRAFT KITS** for each character with directions and supplies to make 3 crafts from the Pastimes Craft Books. Craft Kits are available only through Pleasant Company's catalogue, which you can request by filling out the postcard below.

Turn the page to learn more about the other delights in The American Girls Collection. ⟶

I'm an American girl who loves to get mail. Please send me a catalogue of The American Girls Collection®:

My name is_____

My address is _____

City_____ State _____ Zip _____

Parent's signature_____

And send a catalogue to my friend:

My friend's name is_____

Address _____

City_____ State _____ Zip _____

THE AMERICAN GIRLS COLLECTION®

The American Girls Collection tells the stories of five lively nine-year-old girls who lived long ago—Felicity, Kirsten, Addy, Samantha, and Molly. You can read about their adventures in a series of beautifully illustrated books of historical fiction. By reading these books, you'll learn what growing up was like in times past.

There is also a lovable doll for each character with beautiful clothes and lots of wonderful accessories. The dolls and their accessories make the stories of the past come alive today for American girls like you.

The American Girls Collection is for you if you love to curl up with a good book. It's for you if you like to play with dolls and act out stories. It's for you if you want something so special that you will treasure it for years to come.

To learn more about The American Girls Collection, fill out the postcard on the other side of the page and mail it to Pleasant Company, or call **1-800-845-0005.** We will send you a free catalogue about all the books, dolls, dresses, and other delights in The American Girls Collection.

BUSINESS REPLY MAIL
First Class Mail   Permit No. 1137   Middleton, WI USA

POSTAGE WILL BE PAID BY ADDRESSEE

PLEASANT COMPANY
P.O. Box 620497
Middleton, WI 53562-9940

NO POSTAGE
NECESSARY
IF MAILED
IN THE
UNITED STATES